COLLI
Best Walks
AROUND
FORT WILLIAM

by Richard Hallewell

Illustrations by Rebecca Johnstone

HarperCollins*Publishers*

Published by Collins
An Imprint of HarperCollins*Publishers*
77-85 Fulham Palace Road
London W6 8JB

First published 1998

Copyright © HarperCollins*Publishers* 1998
Maps © Bartholomew 1998

The walks in this guide were first published in
Bartholomew's *Walk Oban, Mull and Lochaber.*

All rights reserved. No part of this publication may be reproduced,
stored in a retrieval system, or transmitted in any form or by any
means, electronic, mechanical, photocopying, recording, or
otherwise, without the prior written permission of the Publisher
and copyright owner.

The landscape is changing all the time. While every care has
been taken in the preparation of this guide, the Publisher accepts
no responsibility whatsoever for any loss, damage, injury or
inconvenience sustained or caused as a result of using this guide.

Printed in Italy

ISBN 0 00 4487109

98/1/17

CONTENTS

Key map for the walks, key to map symbols   4
Introduction   5

Walk		Grade					
Walk 1	Mallaig	B	WC			🚌	10
Walk 2	North Morar	A	WC	👢		🚌	11
Walk 3	Caledonian Canal	B				🚌	12
Walk 4	Glen Roy	B		👢			13
Walk 5	Ben Nevis	A		👢	🐾		14
Walk 6	Glen Nevis	A/B/C		👢			15
Walk 7	Corrychurrachan	C			🐾		16
Walk 8	The Lochan	C	WC		🐾	🚌	17
Walk 9	Devil's Staircase	A	WC	👢		🚌	18
Walk 10	Signal Rock	C	WC		🐾		19
Walk 11	Loch Etive	A/B		👢	🐾		20
Walk 12	Glen Creran to Ballachulish	A	WC	👢		🚌	21
Walk 13	Ariundle	C	WC		🐾	🚌	22
Walk 14	Oakwood Trail	C			🐾		23
Walk 15	Sanna to Portuairk	B		👢			24

Symbols

WC   Public conveniences available at route, or in nearby town. (NB: these facilities are often closed in winter.)

👢   Hill walking equipment required. Strong boots; warm waterproof clothing; map and compass for hill routes.

🐾   Route suitable for dogs.

🚌   Public transport available to this route. Details given on individual routes.

Grade

A   Requires a high level of fitness and – for the hill routes – previous experience of hill walking. The use of a detailed map is advised.

B   Requires a reasonable level of fitness. Book map sufficient.

C   A simple, short walk on good paths.

Key map for the walks

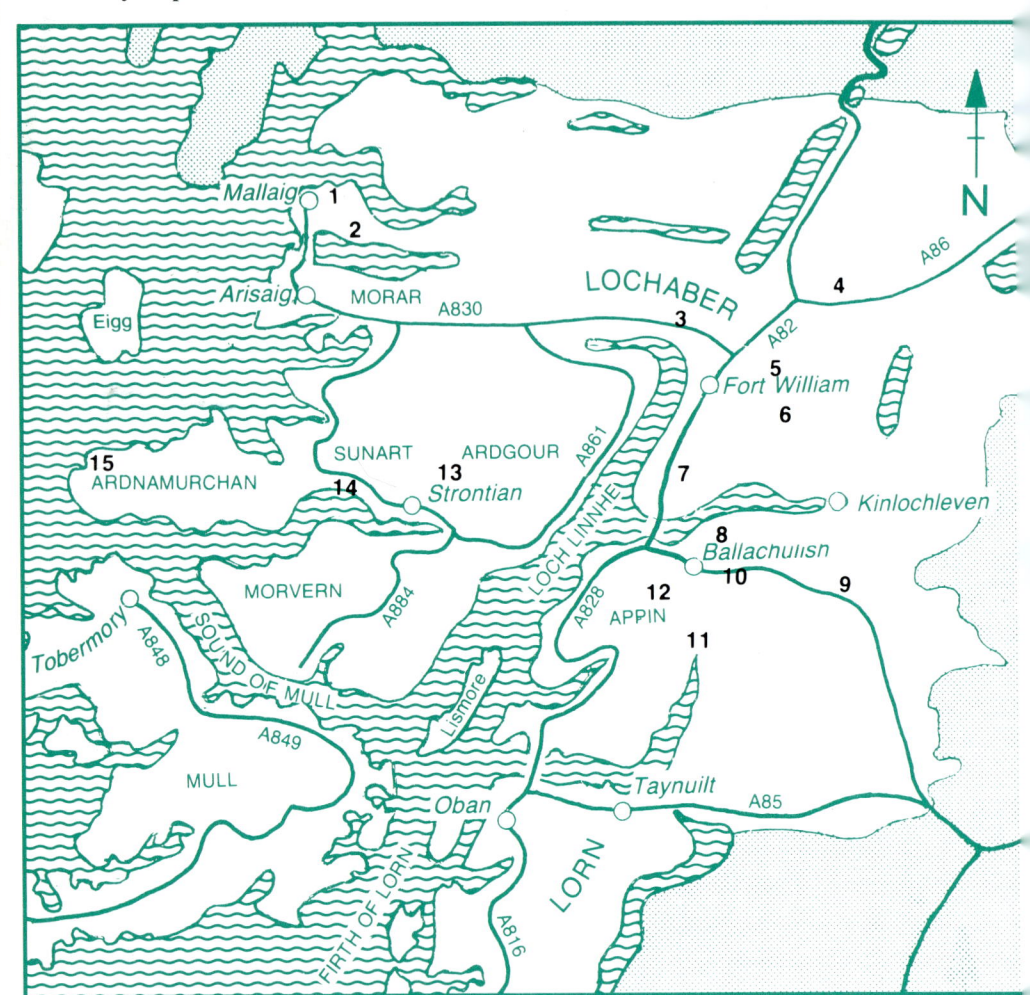

Key to map symbols

- ●●● Route
- === Metalled Road
- ++++ Railway
- Ⓟ Parking
- i Information Centre
- ⌊ Viewpoint
- Marshland
- Moorland
- Coniferous Woodland
- Broad-leaved Woodland
- Contour: shaded area is above height indicated

INTRODUCTION

ABOUT THIS BOOK

This is a book of walks, each of which can be completed within one day. Each route is graded according to its level of difficulty, and wherever specialist hill walking equipment is required this is specified. There is a description of each route, including information on the character and condition of the paths, and with a brief description of the major points of interest along the way. In addition there is a sketch map of the route. Car parks, where available, are indicated on the route maps. The availability of public conveniences and public transport on particular routes is listed on the contents page, and at the head of each route. The suitability or otherwise of the route for dogs is also indicated on the contents page. The location of each route within the area is shown on the key map, and a brief description of how to reach the walk from the nearest town is provided at the start of each walk. National grid references are provided on the maps. The use of a detailed map, in addition to this book, is advised on all grade A walks.

Before setting out, all walkers are asked to read through the section of Advice to Walkers at the end of the Introduction. In the long term it never pays to become lax in taking safety precautions.

THE AREA

(Numbers in italics refer to individual walks.)
This area is famous for its climbing and hill walking, but until the end of the 18th century it was considered far too lawless, and the country too rough, for general travellers. The earliest visitors were inspired by the new craze of Romanticism, which considered the natural world – and the Highlands were undeniably natural – to be the paradigm of beauty.

Ironically, the early travellers – Boswell and Johnson, the Wordsworths and Mendelssohn – were only able to tour the Highlands because of the construction of military roads throughout the area; the purpose of which was to help in the dismantling of the society which had produced the originals of the works they so admired.

Despite these roads, travel was still extremely spartan and travellers remained scarce until the opening of the railways in the 19th century, and the expansion of the terminus towns of Fort William and Oban. In more recent years the improvement of the road system has opened up the area to large numbers of visitors.

The landscape is harsh: high, steep, rocky hills; intersected by narrow glens and long, thin, deep freshwater lochs; the coastline jagged and deeply indented by long sea lochs.

The rocks which form this landscape are largely igneous or metamorphic: granite and basalt, formed by volcanic activity millions of years ago, and carved to their present shape by the glaciers of the ice age.

Following the retreat of the ice the Highlands were gradually colonised by trees, predominantly birch, Scots pine and oak. Only small pockets of these once vast forests remain however: around Loch Tulla, Loch Awe, Loch Creran, Loch Sunart *(13,14)* and South Morar.

Where this forest has been cleared the almost universal cover is of grass or heather moorland. In addition, in recent years, large areas have been given over to plantations of commercial conifers *(7,8,12)*.

The major peaks in the area are Ben More (3169ft/966m) on Mull, Ben Cruachan (3693ft/1126m) by Loch Awe and Ben Nevis (4408ft/1344m) *(5)* – the highest mountain in Britain – to the east of Fort William. In addition, there are virtually continuous ranges throughout the area; notably the hills of Mamore Forest (this term can be misleading; it refers to deer forests, which rarely have any trees at all) to the south of Ben Nevis, the peaks around Beinn Dorain to the east of Glen Orchy, and the great knot of hills to the west of Rannoch Moor, surrounding Glen Etive, Glen Coe and upper Glen Creran *(8-12)*.

The largest of the sea lochs is Loch Linnhe, leading from the southern tip of the Morvern peninsula to Fort William *(3)*, along the glen to Inverness and continuing another ten miles as Loch Eil. Three other major lochs cut east from Linnhe: Loch Etive *(11)*, Loch Creran and Loch Leven. To the west the Sound of Mull cuts between Morvern and the island of Mull. The main lochs to the north of Morvern are Loch Sunart *(13,14)*, the Sound of Arisaig, Loch Nevis *(5)* and Loch Huorn.

The area also contains a number of inland lochs. The largest is Loch Awe (over 20 miles/32km long). The deepest is Loch Morar *(2)*, south of Mallaig.

The close presence of the Atlantic has an effect on the level of precipitation throughout the area; a subject of much interest to walkers. The prevailing westerlies carry a great deal of moisture, which has been picked up crossing the ocean. The air rises as it crosses the high land and deposits great quantities of rain over the hills. As a result, many walks remain damp throughout the year.

Descriptions of the Highlands might suggest an unrelieved landscape of dark mountains shrouded in mist, with white torrents rushing down their flanks into murky lochs. However, the summers are often punctuated by long periods of bright, warm weather, heightened by the reflective power of the ubiquitous lochs and sea lochs. The pure light attracted many late 19th- and early 20th-century painters to the west coast, and particularly to Morar *(1,2)*, Moidart, Ardnamurchan *(15)*, Mull and Iona.

The general cover of the land is of moorland (used as rough grazing for sheep) and forestry, but in places this gives way to patches of fertile soil. Crofting is still common – the crofts are generally composed of a small area of relatively fertile land for crops; backed by rougher land used for grazing animals. In the past crofting was the major source of employment for the people of the area; its limited rewards being augmented by seasonal fishing. Today, many crofters are still involved in fishing, while others have taken to fish farming (the large rafts containing the fish can be seen anchored in many bays along the coast) or tourism.

Much of the land is still owned by large estates, and the high moors are maintained for deer stalking and grouse shooting.

Modern, large-scale industry has not had a particularly rosy history in the Highlands, but there are still aluminium works at Kinlochleven *(9)* and Fort William, and some light industry around Oban and Fort William.

The population is not large, and it has always tended to be scattered in small settlements. During the last two hundred years there has been considerable centralisation, and the main towns have slowly grown, but the population is still largely rural. Services are often far apart along the roads, so it is important to plan well ahead before driving to the remoter corners.

Oban is principally a tourist town, with a commercial edge. Fort William is overshadowed by Ben Nevis and the surrounding peaks. More industrial than Oban, it fills a similar role as service centre to the surrounding glens, and is undoubtedly the hill walkers' and back packers' capital of Scotland

Other main settlements include Mallaig *(1)*: a busy fishing port on the Sound of Sleat; Ballachulish *(12)* on the south side of Loch Leven; and Tobermory.

The area of hills to the west, around Loch Etive, Glen Etive and Glen Coe *(8-11)* are suited to climbing and longer hill walks; as are the hills of Lochaber, east of Fort William *(6,7)*, including Ben Nevis *(5)*. The land north of Mull and the west of the Great Glen – Morvern, Ardnamurchan *(15)*, Ardgour, Sunart *(13,14)*, Moidart, Morar *(1,2)* and Knoydart is also included.

HISTORY

The land is almost empty of physical reminders of the past ages. The Gaelic culture, as all Celtic cultures, has left few visible remains. There are no old towns or palaces where one can guess the nature of past builders; the only monuments the Gaels built were in words: their poems.

Following the ice age, and contemporary with the spread of the great forests, the first people arrived in Scotland from the continent. This initial influx of stone age hunters was followed, over the next nine millennia, by a succession of waves of immigrants who each, in turn, achieved ascendancy over the inhabitants of Scotland and who slowly blended with their predecessors into a hybrid race – the descendants of which are the modern Scots.

The Celts were a widely-spread people who inhabited most of central Europe. After they had been conquered by the Romans on the European mainland their culture quickly vanished, eventually surviving only in those areas on the periphery of Europe – Brittany, Cornwall, Wales, Ireland and Scotland – where the poverty of the land discouraged the Romans from widespread colonisation. In these areas the same lifestyle was followed until the end of the 18th century.

In the early centuries AD there seems to have been a slow colonisation of Argyll by the

Gaels of Ireland (known to the Romans as the Scotti). In 500 AD, Fergus Mór Mac Eirc, the king of Dalriada in Ireland, moved to Argyll. Over the next 350 years his descendents extended their influence over most of mainland Scotland.

There was continual warfare between the new kingdom of Dalriada and the native Picts in the north of Scotland. Eventually Kenneth McAlpin of Dalriada ruled both kingdoms.

The Scots ability to survive was partly due to their ability to call on reinforcements from Ireland, and partly to the moral authority which they held through their guardianship of Iona, the cradle of Scottish Christianity.

Columba, an Irish prince, had founded a community on Iona in 563. In 565 he journeyed up the Great Glen to meet the Pictish king, Brude, at Inverness. His conversion of the king, and the permission he received to spread the Gaelic church – and thus the Gaelic culture – throughout Pictland, signalled the start of the erosion of Pictish culture.

This erosion was completed by the Vikings, who began a series of raids on the British Isles around the end of the 8th century. The Scots and the Picts were driven inland by this mutual foe and gradually became unified under the Gaelic language, church, culture and, in 843, king.

Norse colonisation began around 800, and gradually spread throughout the isles. In 1098 a treaty between King Magnus Bareleg of Norway and King Edgar of Scotland confirmed that the Western Isles, the Isle of Man and Kintyre were under Norwegian sovereignty, where they remained until the mid-13th century, when under the Treaty of Perth of 1266, the land was sold to the Scottish king.

By this time the line of Gaelic/Celtic kings had been superseded by the House of Canmore, which was based upon an Anglo-Norman system and aristocracy, and which maintained close links with the English court. When the line of Canmore ended, with the death of Alexander III in 1286, Scotland was thrown into the turmoil of the Wars of Independence, as first William Wallace and then Robert the Bruce strove to keep Scotland free of English rule.

In the following centuries lowland and Highland Scotland developed separately. The Highlands followed a system similar to that introduced by the Irish into Dalriada, where groups were bound by a real or imagined common ancestry – the clans.

The coinage of the clans was cattle, which proved the only major source of funds to an area which was otherwise largely self-supporting. The export of cattle to the south had been practiced from early times, but it reached its peak in the 18th and 19th centuries, when many thousands of cattle were driven to the great trysts, or cattle markets, at Falkirk and Crieff. Many of the drove roads along which the cattle were driven criss-cross this area; including the Devil's Staircase north from Glen Coe *(9)*, and the track from Inveroran to Tyndrum.

The first powerful clan had been the MacDougalls; who had lost much of their land by opposing Bruce. The subsequent power vacuum was largely filled by the descendants of Angus Og of Islay (chief of the MacDonalds). Inevitably, however, the MacDonalds over extended themselves, threatening the Stewarts (then rulers of Scotland), and their lands were divided amongst clans more loyal to the crown; notably the Campbells.

The next 300 years of history is a catalogue of the murders, battles and deceits which marked the gradual expansion of this great clan at the expense of its neighbours to the north.

The Union of Scotland and England in 1707 had changed the Highlanders from a powerful majority to a dangerous minority – an obvious source of support for the deposed line of the Stewarts.

The lengths to which the Government was prepared to go to keep the peace in the region had been shown by the Massacre of Glen Coe in 1692, in which the MacIan (chief of the MacDonalds of Glen Coe) and 40 or so of his clan were killed by two battalions of the Duke of Argyll's regiment, whom they had been entertaining in the glen for some days. The excuse for the act was that the MacIan had failed to sign an oath of allegiance to the King – whom all the clans were required to officially recognise – by a set date. He had not been the only chief slow to come forward, however, and it was clear that an example was being set. Similarly, there was harsh retribution meted out to the ringleaders after the rising in 1715. Many Highlanders did not care to find out what the response to further trouble might be.

Nonetheless, central authority was resented, and many of the clans had by then little to lose. Thus, the supporters who ralleyed to Charles Stewart after he had landed at Loch nan Uamh, in Moidart, and raised his standard at Glenfinnan, at the head of Loch Shiel (the place is now marked by a monument), were taking a desperate gamble.

The Prince passed through Moidart again, in 1746; this time dodging his pursuers while waiting for the boat which would take him to the continent, following the conclusion of the rising after the rout at Culloden.

In the immediate aftermath of the battle, the Hanoverian army, led by the Duke of Cumberland, acted with some brutality; executing prisoners out of hand and hunting the vanquished forces through the hills. In addition, many of the clansmen were imprisoned or transported; the lands of the Jacobite chiefs were forfeited to the crown, and the Disarming and Disclothing Acts (the latter proscribing the bagpipes and the kilt) were passed.

Within a very short time the Hanoverian chiefs, and those Jacobite chiefs who had been pardoned, were busy raising regiments for the British army. The outstanding service of these regiments created so favourable an impression that before the end of the century the bans were lifted and the forfeited estates returned to their owners.

Much had changed, however. Highland gentlemen, now requiring sufficient funds for the expensive lifestyle of Georgian society opened up to them, raised rents or sought alternative and more renumerative uses for the land. Some local industries were started, such as the iron furnace at Bonawe, and expansion of the fishing industry was encouraged. However, these measures could not cope with the large numbers of people who were being removed from the hills – often forcibly – to make way for sheep. Many of the people left Scotland; either travelling south to work in the new factories of the Industrial Revolution, or emigrating to the expanding Empire, every corner of which is populated by the descendants of the Highlanders.

NATURAL HISTORY

Routes which particularly feature each environment are listed beside the headings, giving a rough indication of the type of thing which may be seen along the way.

Oak and other broad-leaved woodland *(2,3,6,11,13,14).* Following the ice age, much of the Highlands were covered by trees; **Scots pine** and **birch** on the poorer soils and the north facing slopes, and **oak** and other broad-leaved trees on the better soils and the south-facing slopes of the glens. The trees were virtually all felled, for a variety of reasons, and now only fragments remain. Apart from the oak and birch, the woods can include **rowan, hazel, holly, alder, wych elm** and **ash**. The floor of the wood tends to be mossy, with some grass, **blaeberry** and **primrose**. The oaks themselves are often swathed in mosses and lichens, and are sometimes host to climbing **honeysuckle** and **ivy**.

The bird life in these woods is not great – some **warblers** and **finches** may be seen but the shortage of birds limits the range of birds of prey, although those which predominantly prey on small mammals (**buzzard** and **tawny owl**) are likely to be present. The cover of the woods attracts larger mammals: **badger, hedgehog, stoat, weasel, wildcat, fox, roe deer** and, in the north of the area, the **pine marten**. The woods are rich in insect life. The hills of the **wood ant** are common, as are many species of **butterflies, beetles** and **moths**, which in turn provide sustenance to a variety of species of **bats**. In low lying woods plant life can include **wood anemone, foxglove, bluebell, cow wheat, primrose, cranesbill** and **wood garlic**.

Commercial forestry *(7,8,10,12).* These plantations provide cover for **rabbit, fox** and **roe deer**. The trees planted are quite varied and might include not only the native **Scots pine** but also **lodge-pole pine, Sitka** and **Norway spruce, Japanese, European** and **hybrid larch** and **Douglas fir**. The bird life can include **blue, great** and **coal tits, bullfinch** and **chaffinch, crossbill, siskin, jay** and **wood pigeon**.

Mountains and moorland *(4,5,6,9,11,12).* The Highlands are famous for the heather moors, which give a fine purple shade of the hillsides from July to September, but this ground cover is not universal on the hills of the western Highlands. In some areas the moors are floating on a considerable depth of peat, where bogs of dark water often develop. These encourage plants such as **bog cotton, bog asphodel** and **bog myrtle**. The highest peaks are rocky and virtually bare but the **ptarmigan**, the hardiest of the grouse family, might be seen near the tops, or lower in winter. On the lower moors, **black** and **red grouse, stonechat, wheatear** and **curlew** are present, as well as **peregrine, kestrel, golden eagle** and, as everywhere, **hooded crows**. **Red deer** stay high in the hills during the summer, but return to the lower moors during the winter. There are also local colonies of **sika deer** and **wild goats**, and carnivores such as the **wildcat, fox** and **stoat**. The **mountain hare** is rare in this area.

Freshwater *(2,3,6,8)*. The **bog cotton, asphodel** and **myrtle**, and various mosses, reeds and grasses of the moors and peat bogs tend to follow the water courses to the sea's edge throughout this area; only being replaced by woodland flowers where the burns pass through high-sided, narrow glens. Various pondweeds, reeds and sedges grow by the lochs and lochans. The most dramatic of the freshwater birds are the **red-throated** and **black-throated divers** which nest in the high lochans. Also by the upper waters are **redshank, curlew** and **lapwing; dipper** and **grey** and **pied wagtails** are common in the shaded glens. The **otter** is not uncommon throughout the area, though it is quite rare to see one. Other swimmers include **water vole** and **mink**.

Seashore *(1,11,15)*. The most important element on the seashore is the degree of exposure to heavy seas. On exposed beaches the cover is limited to **lichens** and **barnacles**, while, in the sheltered lochs, there is a greater density of **seaweeds**, plus **mussels** and **limpets**. **Crabs** are common between the high and low water marks, while **sea urchins** and **starfish** can be seen just below the lowest tides. The shells of **scallops** and other bivalves are often thrown up along the beaches. Mudflats are rich in **lugworms** and **cockles**, and thus attractive to waders such as the **curlew** and **oyster catcher**. The **common seal** is the mammal most likely to be seen; **otters** can sometimes be seen swimming in the sea, particularly in the evenings. Bird life includes a variety of **gulls** and **terns**, plus **heron, razorbill, guillemot, puffin, cormorant** and **shag; mute** and **whooper swans; eider, teal, tufted duck, wigeon** and other ducks. Waders include **curlew, oyster catcher, dunlin, redshank, sandpiper** and others. There has been a gradual increase in the number of **sea eagles** along the coast; stemming from an original group released on Rum.

ADVICE TO WALKERS

Always check the weather forecast before setting off on the longer walks and prepare yourself for the walk accordingly. Remember that an excess of sunshine – causing sunburn or dehydration – can be just as debilitating as snow or rain, and carry adequate cover for your body in all conditions when on the hills.

Snow cover on higher slopes often remains well into the summer and should be avoided by inexperienced walkers as it often covers hidden watercourses and other pitfalls which are likely to cause injury. Also soft snow is extremely gruelling to cross and can sap energy quickly. Walking on snow-covered hills should not be attempted without an ice axe and crampons.

The other weather-associated danger on the hills is the mist, which can appear swiftly and cut visibility to a few yards. A map and compass should be carried while on the higher hills.

Obviously these problems are unlikely to arise on the shorter, simpler routes, but it is always wise when out walking to anticipate the worst and to be ready for it. The extra equipment may never be needed, but it is worth taking anyway, just in case. Spare food, a first aid kit, a whistle and a torch with a spare battery should be carried on all hill walks. In addition, details of your route and expected time of return should be left with someone, who you should advise on your safe return.

From August onwards there is grouse shooting and deer stalking on the moors. If you are undertaking one of the hill routes, first check with the local estate or tourist office, thereby avoiding a nuisance for the sportsmen and possible danger to yourself.

COUNTRY CODE

All walkers, when leaving public roads to pass through farmland, forestry or moorland, should respect the interests of those whose livelihood depends on the land. Carelessness can easily cause damage. You are therefore urged to follow the Country Code:

Guard against all risk of fire.

Keep all dogs under proper control (especially during the lambing season — April and May).

Fasten all gates.

Keep to the paths across farmland.

Avoid damaging fences, hedges and walls.

Leave no litter.

Safeguard water supplies.

Protect wildlife, wild plants and trees.

Go carefully on country roads.

Respect the life of the countryside.

1 Mallaig

Length: 4 miles (6.5km)
Height climbed: 300ft (90m)
Grade: B
Public conveniences: Mallaig
Public transport: Rail service between Mallaig and Fort William

A short walk along the coast on public roads and a rough track; back over a low hill. Splendid views of the islands to the west.

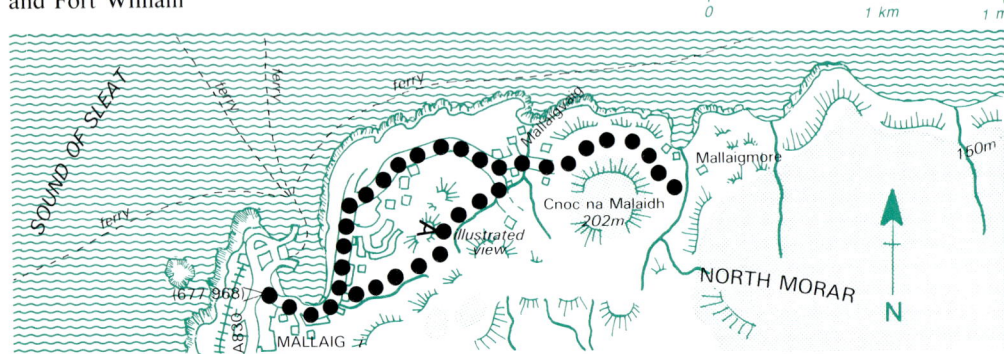

Mallaig is an important fishing harbour and a ferry terminus for Skye and the Small Isles. It is neither old (there was little on the site before this century) nor particularly pretty, but it has that vitality peculiar to working harbours, and occupies a most dramatic position on the edge of North Morar; looking out beyond the Hebrides to the Atlantic. The town is the northern terminus of the West Highland railway (running from Glasgow, through Fort William) and also marks the conclusion of the A830 road north from Fort William.

Park in Mallaig and walk around the head of the bay. Beyond the town continue around the point to the hamlet of Mallaigvaig. From here a rough path cuts along a steep slope, around the coast to the bay at Mallaigmore. From this track there are fine views across Loch Nevis to the mountains of Knoydart.

Double back to Mallaigvaig and follow the signposted track to the left, up a small glen, across a low pass and back down into Mallaig. To the right of this path there is a low hill, from which there are splendid views.

1. *Eigg* 2. *Mallaig* 3. *Rum* 4. *Sleat* 5. *Sound of Sleat* 6. *Cuillin Hills*

10

2 North Morar

Length: 8 miles (13.5km)
Height Climbed: Negligible
Grade: A
Public conveniences: Mallaig
Public transport: Morar Station on rail link between Fort William and Mallaig

A long walk by the side of a large inland loch, on a quiet public road and a rough track. Back by the same route, or around the coast by ferry.

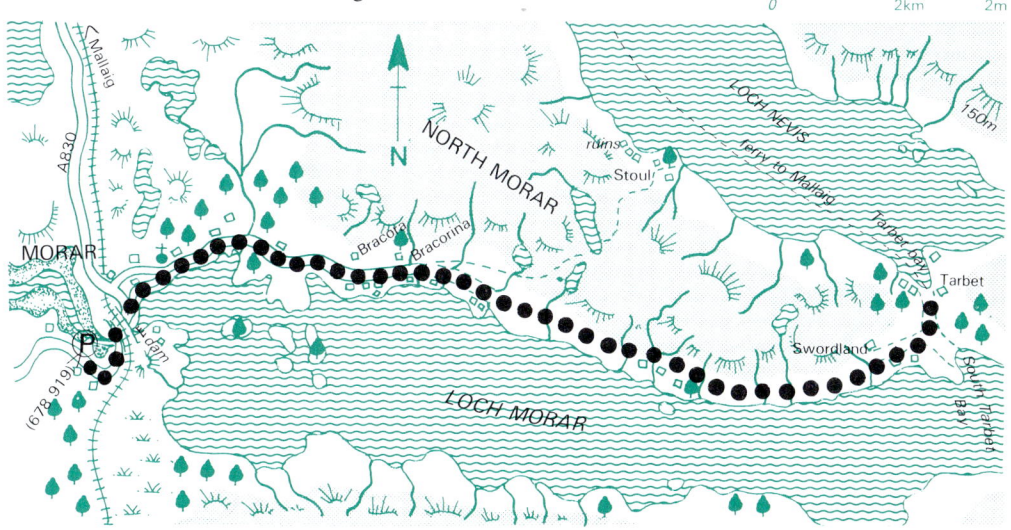

This walk makes use of an occasional ferry service, running from Mallaig, up Loch Nevis to Tarbet. If it is intended to use this for the return route then check ferry times (contact ferry operators through Mallaig Tourist Information Centre) and allow around 3 hours for the walk.

To reach Morar, drive north on the A830 road from Fort William to Mallaig. Park in Morar, 2 miles south of Mallaig, beautifully situated by a white, sandy inlet across which the River Morar meanders.

Walk along the minor road to the east, by the north shore of Loch Morar. The loch is 17 miles long and, off Swordland, the water is over 1000ft deep. At the shallow western end there are a number of pleasant, wooded islands. On one of these there was a Catholic seminary, which was destroyed after the Battle of Culloden in 1746.

After 3 miles the road degenerates into a track, which quickly splits into two divergent paths. One leads over the hill to the north, to the little abandoned settlement of Stoul. The other (the path for this route) continues along the shore. The slope down to the water is very steep in places, and the rough path curves around the headlands above the loch, giving fine views of the mass of peaks at the eastern end of the loch, and westwards, across the wooded islands to the mountains of the island of Rum.

Continue on this path, past the Victorian shooting-lodge at Swordland. A short distance beyond the lodge the track splits. Cut hard left, through a narrow pass and down to the shore of Tarbet Bay on the sea-loch, Loch Nevis.

3 Caledonian Canal

Length: 4 miles (7km)
Height Climbed: Negligible
Grade: B
Public conveniences: None
Public transport: Bus service from Fort William

A leisurely stroll along a canal towpath, and back along a quiet public road. Fine view of Ben Nevis.

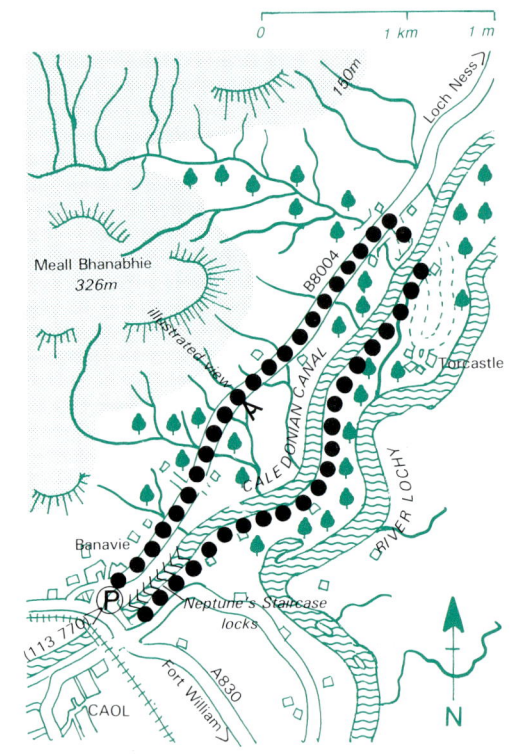

The Caledonian Canal was surveyed by Thomas Telford at the start of the 19th century, and finally completed in 1847; shortening the long trip around Scotland's north coast. The canal runs from Inverness, on the Moray Firth, to Corpach, just north of Fort William. It was intended as an aid to fishing and trading vessels, but is now largely used by pleasure craft.

Drive north from Fort William and turn left onto the road to Mallaig; then right, after crossing the canal, into the car park at Banavie.

At this point the canal climbs through a series of locks known as 'Neptune's Staircase'. Start walking up the eastern side of the canal.

After 2 miles a path drops down from the towpath, just before some cottages to the right of the canal. Turn down this and double back through a charming arch beneath the canal. Where this path joins the B8004 turn left to return to Banavie. Along this road there are tremendous views to the south-east of Ben Nevis and the surrounding peaks.

1. Aonach Mór (1219m) **2.** Carn Mór Dearg (1223m) **3.** Ben Nevis (1344m)
4. Carn Dearg (1211m) **5.** Meall an t-Suidhe (708m) **6.** Mullach nan Coirean (938m)
7. Cow Hill **8.** Inverlochy Castle Hotel **9.** Caledonian Canal **10.** Aluminium Works

12

4 Glen Roy

Length: 5 miles (8km)
Height Climbed: 400ft (120m)
Grade: B
Public conveniences: None
Public transport: None

A brisk walk through an area of great geological interest. The going is generally rough, through the thick heather moorland on the hill sides.

The most interesting features of Glen Roy are its 'Parallel Roads': a series of sloping ridges, running the length of the glen at a uniform height. These were formed during the latter part of the ice age, when a loch formed in the glen, dammed by a glacier in Glen Spean. As the glacier deteriorated, over a long period, the loch was held at different levels. The parallel roads mark the beaches which formed along the strand of this loch. This route follows the line of one such strand.

To reach Glen Roy drive north from Fort William on the A82. Turn onto the A86 at Spean Bridge and drive 3 miles to Roybridge. Turn left at the village, up Glen Roy. There is a car park 3 miles up the glen.

A rough path runs directly up the slope of Bohuntine Hill behind the car park, across the lowest of the parallel roads, at 857ft/261m, and on up to the next at 1068ft/326m. From here the lines of the roads are visible along the sides of the upper glen.

Walk north along the road, turning sharply around the northern end of Bohuntine Hill and continuing along the damp slopes of Glen Collarig. The line of the road disappears along this section, and at the southern end of the hill there are large conifer plantations. Cut up to the left at the conifers, across the level moorland of Meall Dubh, and down the far side to rejoin the parallel road. Follow this back to the car park.

One famous visitor to the glen was the Marquess of Montrose, who, at the height of his brief, brilliant career, led a small Royalist army over the snow-filled passes at the head of the glen in 1645, on his way to surprise and defeat the Duke of Argyll at Inverlochy.

5 Ben Nevis

Length: Up to 11 miles (18km) to summit and back
Height climbed: 4400ft (1330m)
Grade: A
Public conveniences: None
Public transport: None

A rough, gruelling hill climb up Britain's highest peak. Views outstanding, weather permitting.

To reach the foot of the path up Ben Nevis drive north from the centre of Fort William and then cut right to follow one of the two minor roads up Glen Nevis. There are car parks on either (see map).

The great, rounded granite mass of Ben Nevis is the highest hill in Great Britain, and, during the summer, a large number of people trek slowly along the path up its west ridge. Sadly, it is not the most fascinating of climbs, and the doleful procession of walkers along the long incline gives the impression of a mass act of penitence. Nonetheless, it is a pleasant thing to have done, and the views - when they can be seen - are superb.

A few points should be made about the climb. Firstly, do make sure that you are sensibly attired for the conditions at the top of the hill, as well as for those at the bottom. Its very height ensures that it will be cold (even in mid-summer there are often pockets of snow near the summit) and the omnipresent wind adds to the chill. In addition, the path is very rough and it is foolish not to wear thick hill-walking boots for the climb. On those rare days when the peak is free of cloud it is still important to keep covered up: at this height the sun burns very easily.

There should be no trouble following the path, which cuts deeply into the hillside below Meall an t-Suidhe, but be aware that the round contours of the southern face are not repeated to the north, where there are cliffs of well over 1000ft, and be sure to stick to the path (marked by a series of cairns across the rocky ground near the summit) in thick weather.

6 Glen Nevis

Length: Up to 30 Miles (48km), to Corrour and back
Height climbed: 350ft (100m), to Steall
Grade: A/B/C
Public conveniences: None
Public transport: None

A long, lineal track; leading through a narrow, wooded gorge to a broad, flat, upper valley. Tremendous scenery.

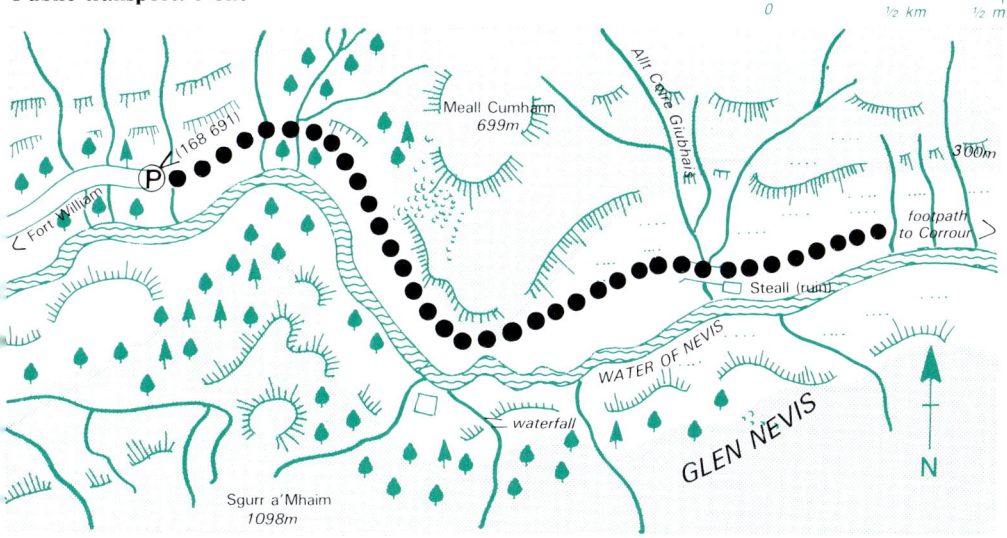

This is a long, lineal route which leads, ultimately, to Corrour Station (but only after a gruelling trek which should not be attempted without detailed maps, etc). Perhaps the most dramatic scenery, however, is along the first two miles (ie, as far as the ruin at Steall).

To reach the walk, drive to the northern end of Fort William and follow the signs for Glen Nevis. A quiet road leads up, through this narrow glen, hemmed in by tall hills and with a scattering of woodland along the river, to a car park at the end of the road. To the north of the car park sheets of water run down the smooth rock face of a southern spur of Ben Nevis. A sign indicates the start of the path.

The track is quite clear, running along the side of a wooded gully through which the Water of Nevis pours, zig-zagging between Meall Cumhann and the northern buttress of Sgurr a'Mhaim. The wood – of Scots pine, birch, sallow, rowan and others – is thick on the steep slopes, and the path runs along a narrow ledge; sometimes overhung by cliffs. At first the river can only be heard, rumbling amongst the rocks below, but further on, where it rises to the level of the path, the way in which the cliffs and rocks have been carved by the water can be seen.

The gorge lasts for about $1/2$ mile, after which the path rounds an outcrop of rock and a broader glen, through which the river slowly meanders, comes to view. Down the hill on the far side of the glen there is an impressive waterfall.

The path becomes less clear now, and the going damper. The trees end and the moorland begins. Walk as far as you wish and then double back to the car park.

7 Corrychurrachan

Length: 2 miles (3km)
Height climbed: 200ft (70m)
Grade: C
Public conveniences: None
Public transport: None

A short, signposted forestry trail on clear tracks. Views of upper Loch Linnhe.

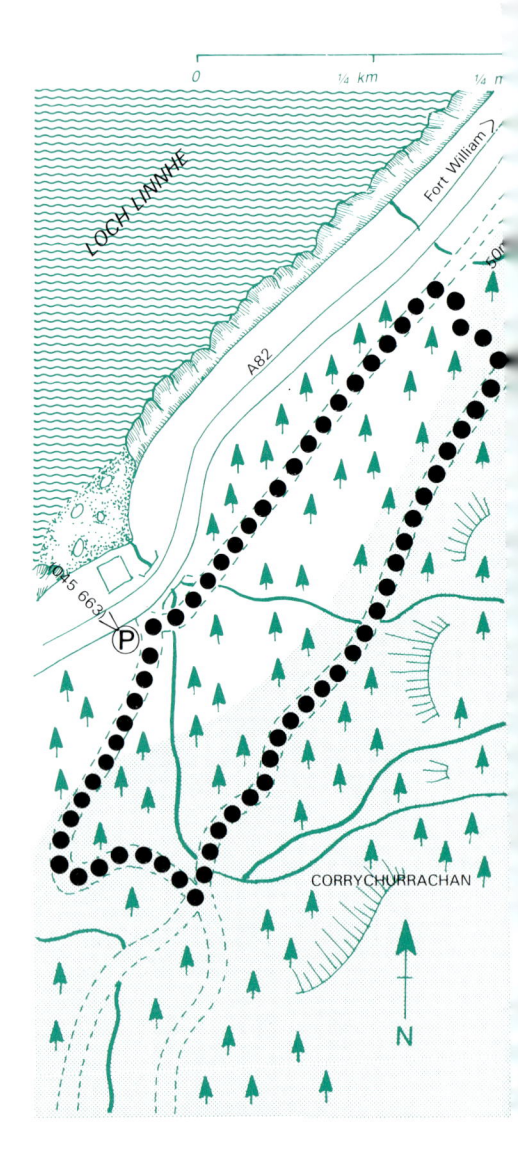

This is a staight-forward forest walk, along Forestry Commission tracks through thick conifer plantations which are planted along the lower slopes of the most westerly hills of Lochaber, butted against the shore of Loch Linnhe: a long sea-inlet which stretches from Fort William down to Mull. From the high section of this path there are good views across upper Loch Linnhe to shallow Inverscaddle Bay, backed by the hills of Ardgour. Down the loch are the Corran narrows, across which the car ferry runs to Ardgour, Morvern and Ardnamurchan.

To reach Corrychurrachan from Fort William, head south from the town on the A82 road, and drive 6 miles along Loch Linnhe until a sign indicates a car park for the walk, up to the left.

Walk north out of the car park and follow a broad track through the trees along the steep side of Beinn Bhan. After a short distance a rough path leads up to the right, zig-zagging through young trees to join another track, further up the hill.

Turn right along this track, which eventually doubles back to the car park.

8 The Lochan

Length: 2 miles (3km)
Height climbed: Negligible
Grade: C
Public conveniences: Glencoe village
Public transport: Bus service from Oban and Fort William

A short forest trail through mixed woodland around a small loch. Fine views of surrounding mountain and coastal scenery.

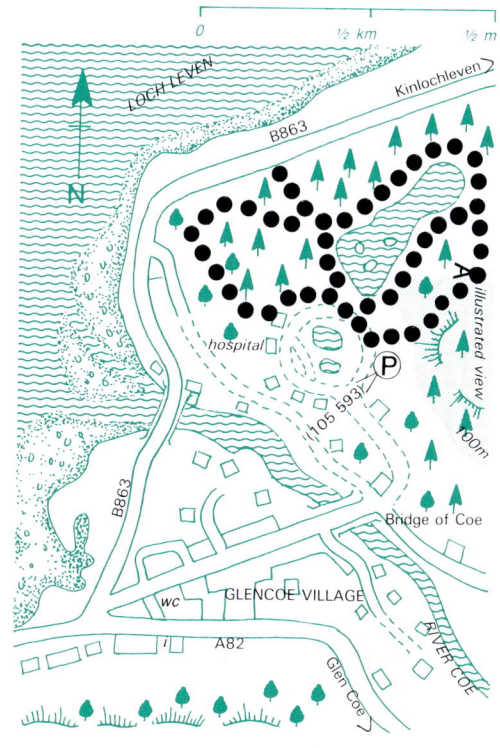

The Lochan trail provides a number of short paths through a very pleasant and varied conifer and broad-leaved plantation, with a track around a small lochan, and good views (see below) from vantage points above Loch Leven. The paths are very clear and generally dry.

To reach the walk drive to Glencoe village - at the western end of Glen Coe, on the A82 Fort William to Glasgow road - and follow the main street, eastwards, over the bridge across the River Coe. Just beyond the bridge turn left, up the drive to the hospital. When the drive forks take the right-hand track, which leads up to the car park.

To the east of the plantation is the prominent mound of Sgurr na Ciche, the Pap of Glen Coe; the most westerly peak on the north side of the glen. To the west the views down Loch Leven are extensive. In the loch there are two small islands. The wooded island is Eilean Munde *(the Island of Mundis)* on which there are the remains of a church. The grassy island is Eilean Choinneich *(the Island of Meetings)* and was a neutral meeting place where clan disputes were resolved.

1. Sgorr Dhearg (1024m) **2.** Ballachulish **3.** Creag Ghorm **4.** Loch Leven
5. Creach Bheinn (853m) **6.** Garbh Bheinn (885m) **7.** Loch Linnhe **8.** Ballachulish Bridge
9. Eilean Munde **10.** Eilean Choinneich **11.** Creag Bhreac

9 Devil's Staircase

Length: 6 miles (9.5km) one way
Height climbed: 1800ft (550m) north to south; 900ft (270m) south to north
Grade: A
Public conveniences: Kinlochleven
Public transport: Kinlochleven to Glencoe bus

An old track across moor-covered hills. The route is generally clear and there are excellent views of the surrounding hills.

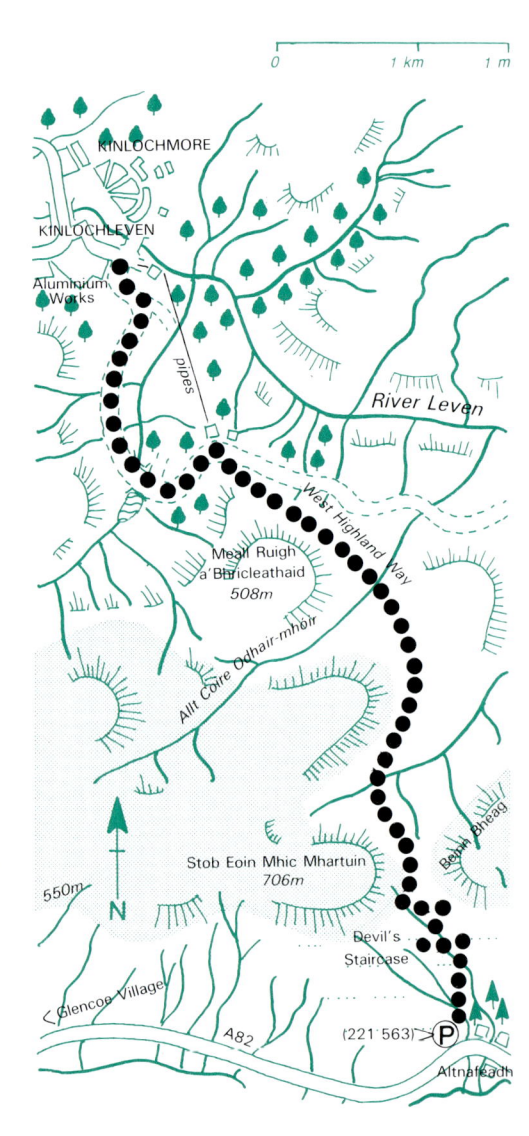

The 'Devil's Staircase' is the name given to a steep, zig-zagging section of the hill-path leading from the eastern end of Glen Coe to Kinlochleven to the north. The path was originally a military road, built in the mid-18th century as part of the grand plan for the supression of the Highlands after the Jacobite uprisings.

Park at Altnafeadh; across the River Coupall from the great bulk of Buachaille Etive Mór; the hill which marks the eastern entrance to Glen Coe from Rannoch Moor. The path is signposted and starts just to the west of Altnafeadh, climbing slowly across damp moorland before the slope steepens approaching the col between Stob Eoin Mhic Mhartuin and Beinn Bheag. The track then cuts back and forth across the slope, quickly climbing to the dip between the hills, from where there are splendid views of the rugged peaks to the south, and a distant sighting of the rounded bulk of Ben Nevis, across the hills of Mamore Forest to the north.

The track now crosses a wide heathery corrie and cuts round a low ridge before dropping again to cross Allt Coire Odhair-mhóir. To the east the Blackwater Reservoir is visible. This is the main power source for the aluminium works at Kinlochleven. Down in the narrow glen of the River Leven there is extensive broad-leaved woodland.

The path joins a more permanent track and drops down towards the town, making a wide detour to cross the bridge over the Allt Coire Mhorair. To the right, alongside this final section, are the great pipes which carry the water down to the works.

10 Signal Rock

Length: 1½ miles (2.5km)
Height climbed: Negligible
Grade: C
Public conveniences: Information centre
Public transport: None

A number of clear, signposted tracks through mixed woodland in the heart of mountainous Glen Coe.

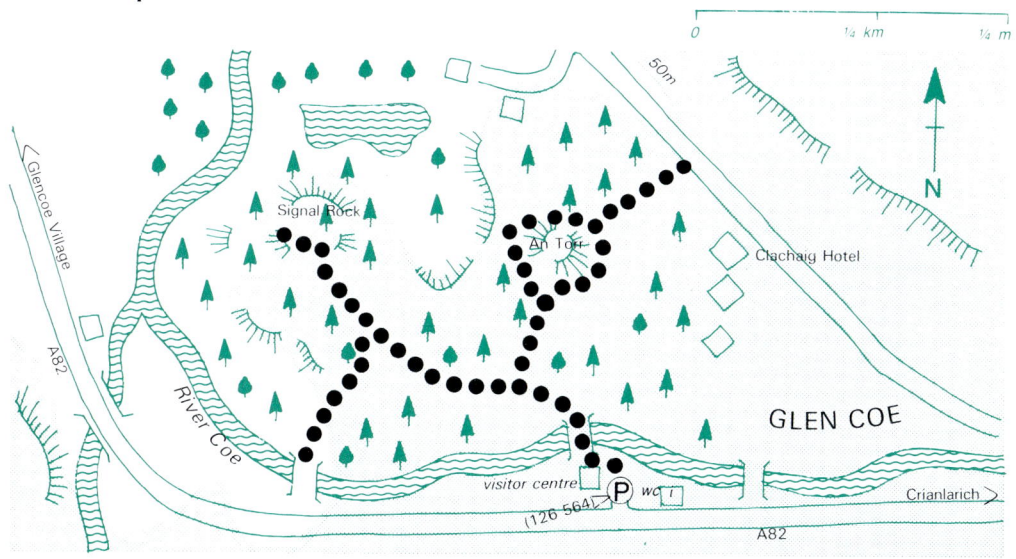

Signal Rock sits amongst the woods in a crook in the River Coe, where Glen Coe bends to the north, about 2 miles south-east of Glencoe village. From the top of this abrupt, rocky hillock can be seen (or could be seen, before the trees grew up around it) the greater part of the glen. This useful vantage point was used by the people of the glen as a signal station. Also, it is traditionally believed to be the point from which the command was given - most probably by lighting a large bonfire - at the start of the Massacre of Glen Coe, on the morning of 14th February, 1692. The cold-blooded murder of the MacDonalds of Glen Coe by their guests - soldiers of the Duke of Argyll's regiment; commanded by Robert Campbell of Glen Lyon, and under the orders of King William - is one of the most reprehensible and depressing acts in British history.

There is an information centre in the glen, from which the walk to the loch begins. The paths, largely through conifers, with some broad-leaved woodland interspersed, are clearly signposted and provide dry walking.

The scenery in this area is some of the most dramatic in the Highlands; with towering, steep, rocky peaks surrounding the narrow glen. To the north of the rock is Sgurr nam Fiannaidh *(the Peak of the Fiann)*; a reference to the legendary Irish warriors who fought under Finn MacCumhaill, and who are associated, in old tales, with many places throughout the Highlands. To the south is the broad Gleann Leac na Muidhe and the grey faces of An t-Sròn *(the Nose)* and Aonach Dubh *(Black Slope)*, on which is Ossian's Cave; traditionally believed to have been the retreat of Finn's bardic son.

11 Loch Etive

Length: Any distance, up to 11 miles (17.5km) to Bonawe (one way)
Height climbed: Negligible
Grade: A/B
Public conveniences: None
Public transport: None

A rough, damp lineal path running by the side of a long sea-loch. Moorland, conifers and broad-leaved woodland along the way.

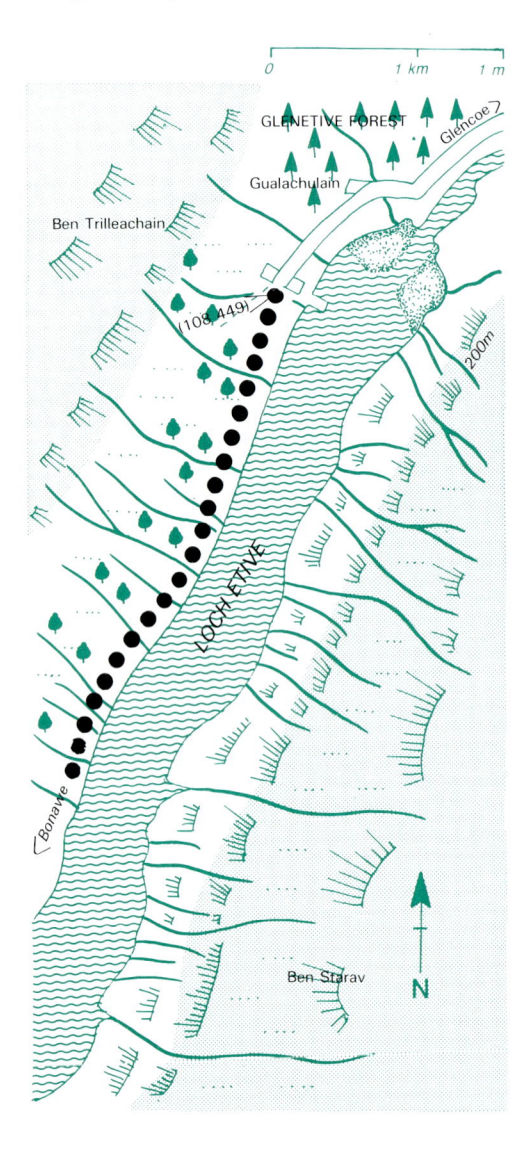

Loch Etive is a long, thin sea-loch; winding some 18 miles from the churning, tidal Falls of Lora under the Connel Bridge, at the mouth of the loch, back into the high hills. For most of its length the loch is inaccessible except on foot. There are rough footpaths along both sides of the loch.

To reach the head of Loch Etive, drive to the eastern end of Glen Coe and turn off the A82 around the eastern end of Buachaille Etive Mór *(the Herdsman of Etive)*, down the minor road signposted to the glen. It is some 13 miles down this single-track road to the head of the loch.

Where the road ends there is an open area for parking, by an old pier. Start walking along a faint, rough and very wet footpath which leads down the west side of the loch. The cover at the upper end of the loch is a mixture of open moorland and patches of mixed woodland: birch, holly, rowan, ash and oak.

The surrounding hills are composed entirely of granite, and fall steeply on either side of the upper loch. To the west is Beinn Trilleachan, with its great water-washed slabs set into the hillside, and to the east is Ben Starav.

This path continues for 11 miles down to Bonawe.

12 Glen Creran to Ballachulish

Length: 7 miles (11km) one way
Height climbed: 1200ft (370m) either way
Grade: A
Public conveniences: Ballachulish
Public transport: Ballachulish on bus route between Oban and Fort William

A steep hill climb, partly through thick forestry. Excellent mountain scenery. Possible alternative route to Duror.

To reach Glen Creran from Oban, drive 5 miles north, on the A85, to the Connel Bridge, and turn onto the A828 road towards Fort William. Just beyond the bridge at the head of Loch Creran a minor road cuts to the right. Follow this to its conclusion at Elleric car park.

From the car park there are two tracks. Take the left-hand track (the right-hand leads up Glen Ure: the home of Colin Campbell, the victim of the Appin Murder in 1746).

The track starts through mixed woodland, which quickly gives way to dense conifer forestry. After 1½ miles the track splits. Take the left-hand route, which climbs steeply, up into the high hills around the head of Glen Creran. Note the pieces of slate in the soil along the track. The seams of high-quality slate through these hills were profitably quarried at Ballachulish from as early as 1761, and the extraction continued until recent times.

1½ miles beyond the split the main track ends and an older, rougher track continues climbing steeply through the forest; finally breaking out of the trees on the narrow col between Fraochaidh and Sgorr a'Choise. From the col there are splendid views of the surrounding peaks; notably the scree slopes of Beinn a'Bheithir, directly ahead.

Climb over the stile on the col and follow the small glen beyond, down towards Gleann an Fhiodh. There is no clear path in the upper part of the glen; aim to cross to a cairn on the hill opposite. From this cairn one path cuts upstream, before Beinn a'Bheithir, leading 5½ miles to Duror. Downstream the path leads to Ballachulish village by Loch Leven.

21

13 Ariundle

Length: 4 miles (6.5km)
Height Climbed: 350ft (100m)
Grade: C
Public conveniences: Strontian
Public transport: Occasional bus service from Fort William

Short, lineal route through a natural oak-wood. Paths good.

Strontian and the straggling line of settlements spreading 2 miles up the valley to the north were built to house the miners in the local lead mines, first brought into production in the early 18th century. The village gave its name to Strontium, a metal found in the mineral Strontianite, first discovered in the lead mines. The mines are closed now (their remains can still be seen beside the road to Polloch) but the hills behind Strontian hold another valuable commodity: a Highland oak wood, of the type which once covered much of the western Highlands.

To reach Strontian drive south from Fort William to Corran Ferry, on the A82. Take the ferry across the narrows and then turn left, down the A861, for 13 miles to Strontian, at the head of the long inlet of Loch Sunart. Turn right at the north end of the village, up a minor road. After 1 mile the road forks. Follow the right-hand track, ½ mile to the car park.

The route is clear: along a good track on the side of the glen of the Strontian River and back by the same route, through an area now maintained as a Nature Reserve. The wood is largely of oak trees, swathed in a rich mass of mosses and lichens, but there are also birch, rowan, ash, alder and others. Typically, for a northern oak wood, the wood is very quiet; rich in insects but poor in birds. The mammals present include otter, fox, wild cat, pine marten and roe deer; only the latter of which is likely to be seen.

This wood owes its survival to the management of the charcoal burners of the 18th and 19th centuries, who supplied oak charcoal for the iron works on Loch Etive.

4 Oakwood Trail

Length: 1 mile (2km)
Height Climbed: Negligible
Grade: C
Public conveniences: None
Public transport: None

A short, signposted walk through natural woodland on a promontory above a sea-loch. Fine views of the surrounding hills. Paths clear.

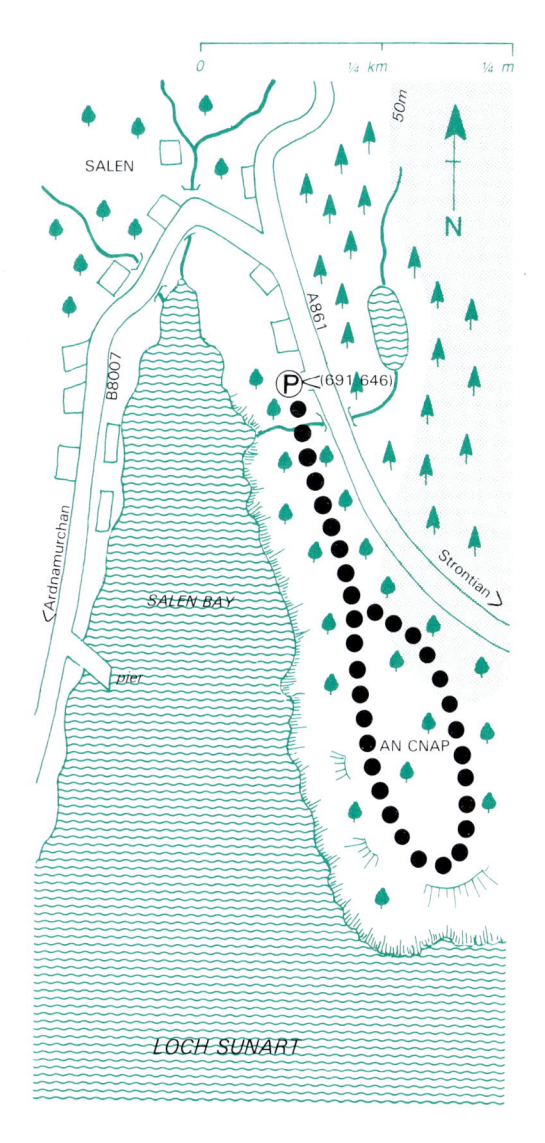

This is a very short walk, through a patch of oakwood to the east of Salen Bay.

To reach Salen, drive south from Fort William to Corran Ferry; take the ferry across the narrow neck of Loch Linnhe and turn left along the A861. It is 23 miles along this road to the little village; built around the head of an inlet of Loch Sunart, at the junction of the A861 with the B8007 Ardnamurchan road.

A little before the village there is a small car park beside the road. Park here and start walking along a clear track. The route follows a short loop, passing a viewpoint on the promontory above Salen Bay and doubling back to the car park. The views are dramatic and extensive: down Loch Sunart and across the water to the hills of Morvern.

The cover in this wood is broad-leaved and predominantly of oak trees; a type of woodland which once clothed the south-facing slopes of most of the west Highland glens. There is comparatively little bird life in these woods, but they are rich in mosses, lichens and insects. Plant life includes honeysuckle, primrose, wood anemone and cow wheat.

There is a variety of animal life in the oakwoods, but it is generally either small - mice, voles and shrews - or largely nocturnal, such as the fox, wild cat, badger and pine marten. The only mammals which are likely to be seen are roe deer - particularly early in the morning - or, in the evening, the bats which feed on the wide variety of insects which inhabit the oak woods.

15 Sanna to Portuairk

Length: 2 miles (3km) there and back
Height Climbed: 150ft (40m)
Grade: B
Public conveniences: None
Public transport: None

A short walk through coastal moorland and sand dunes. Possible extensions. Rough in places.

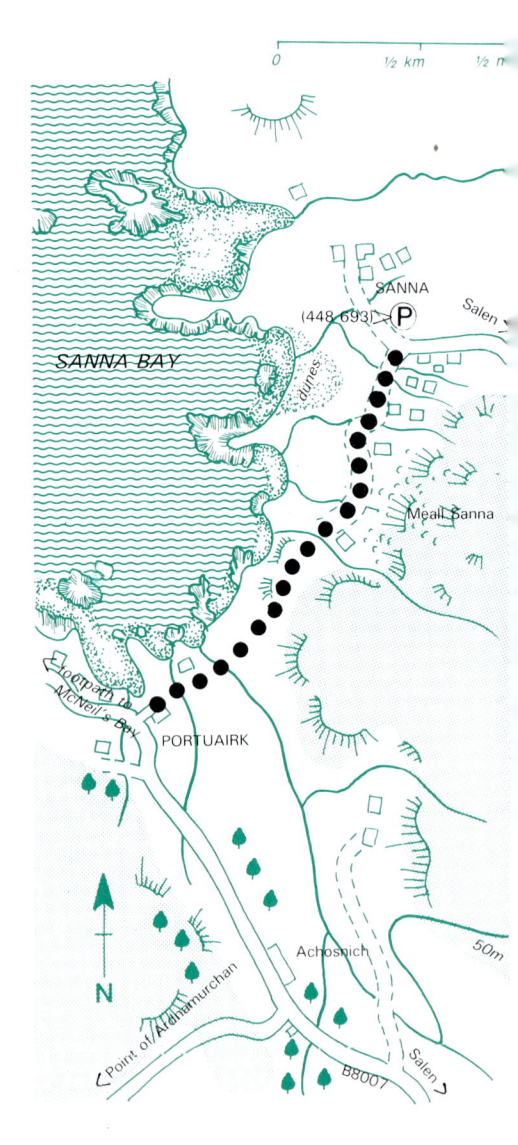

The promontory of Ardnamurchan is some 18 miles long, from the little village of Salen on Loch Sunart to the the headland ot Corrachadh Mòr: the most westerly point of mainland Britain. To anyone uninitiated in the joys of Highland, single-track roads it will seem every inch of this distance and more, as the road winds through the great empty expanses of rocky moorland. Leave plenty of time for the trip.

To reach Ardnamurchan follow the Mallaig road from Fort William and turn south, onto the A861, as far as Salen. At this point turn onto the B8007. Follow the signs for Sanna; a small crofting community by a wide sandy bay near the point of Ardnamurchan.

In the midst of such a vast, empty area there scarcely seems any point in mentioning a single route; the area is so clearly perfect for long hill walks. Indeed, outside the stalking season, when it is best to stay off the hills, there is no reason why well-equipped, experienced walkers should not set off at almost any point. However, the coast along this stretch has developed into a number of pleasant sandy bays, and the views across the water - of Coll to the south-east; Muck, Eigg and Rum to the north-west - are tremendous.

Park at Sanna and walk south, through the dunes. To the left is Meall Sanna; not high, but craggy and, like much of Ardnamurchan, largely scraped free of soil by the glaciers of the ice age.

Where the beach ends cut inland over a rocky ridge, then drop down again - there is no clear path - across a small burn surrounded by wild iris, and on into the hamlet of Portuairk.